COUNTRY FACT FILES

Brazil

Marion Morrison

MACDONALD YOUNG BOOKS

First published in 1994 by Simon & Schuster Young Books
© Simon & Schuster Young Books 1994. Reprinted in 1996 and
1997 by Macdonald Young Books

Macdonald Young Books, an imprint of Wayland Publishers Ltd
61 Western Road
Hove
East Sussex
BN3 1JD

Design	Roger Kohn
Editor	Diana Russell
DTP editor	Helen Swansbourne
Picture research	Valerie Mulcahy
Illustration	Malcolm Porter
	János Márffy
Consultant	David Barrs
Commissioning editor	Debbie Fox

We are grateful to the following for permission
to reproduce photographs:
Front Cover: Magnum (Burt Glinn) *above*, Eye Ubiquitous/TRIP
(Julia Waterlow) *below;* Allsport, page 25 (David Cannon);
Colorific!, pages 16–17 (Claus C Meyer); Sue
Cunningham/Sue Cunningham Photographic, pages 11 *above*,
18 *below*, 22, 23, 27 *below*, 29 *above*, 38, 43; Index/South
American Pictures, page 12; Roger Kohn, pages 34 *above*,
35 *right*; Tony Morrison/South American Pictures, pages 8, 9,
11 *below*, 13, 14, 15, 16 *left*, 18–19, 20, 21, 24, 26, 27 *above*,
29 *below*, 31, 32, 33, 34 *below*, 35 *left*, 36, 37, 39, 41, 42;
Zefa, page 30.

The statistics given in this book are the most up to date
available at the time of going to press

Printed in Hong Kong by Wing King Tong Co Ltd

A CIP catalogue record for this book is available from
the British Library

ISBN: 0 7500 1329 X

**C
O
N
T
E
N
T
S**

Words that are explained in the glossary are printed in
SMALL CAPITALS the first time they are mentioned in the text.

◼ INTRODUCTION

Ask anyone what they know about Brazil and most people will mention the Amazon River, the rainforest and its destruction, which has been so much in the news during the last few years. Others may say coffee, Carnival and Rio de Janeiro's Copacabana beach.

Most will mention football, for Brazil has won the World Cup three times, or Grand Prix racing since the recent triumphs of Nelson Piquet and Ayrton Senna. But although Brazil is well known for all these things, many of them fun-loving, there is much, much more to this huge country.

Huge is the correct word, for Brazil is the world's fifth largest country. Only Russia, Canada, China and the

◀ *Carnival involves over 20,000 dancers and lasts 2 days and nights in February or March. Here dancers in national colours celebrate Brazil's love of football.*

USA have more territory. Brazil also has the fifth largest population in the world, but its population is not increasing as fast as in most of the developing world. However, although Brazil is almost 35 times larger than the UK, it has only three times as many inhabitants.

Brazil is the giant of South America. It is so vast that it shares frontiers with all except two of the 12 countries that make up the

▼ In rural Brazil there are many poor and unemployed. Outside this snack-bar in the north-east, people sell sweetcorn cooked on a homemade metal grill.

- Area: 8,511,996 km
- Population: 1991: 153,322 million
- Density: 18 people per sq kilometre
- Capital and population: Brasília, 1.8 million
- Other main cities and population:
  São Paulo 9.7 million
  Rio de Janeiro 5.5 million
  Belo Horizonte 2.1 million
  Salvador 2 million
  Porto Alegre 1.3 million
  Recife 1.3 million
  Belém 1.2 million
  Manaus 0.9 million
- Highest mountain: Pico da Neblina, 3,014 metres
- Language: Portuguese
- Main religion: Catholic
- Currency: New real
- Economy: Increasingly industrialized
- Major resources: minerals, coal, oil, timber, rivers
- Major products: coffee, soya and soya products, sugar, rubber, textiles, footwear, paper, motor vehicles, electrical and electronic goods, minerals
- Environmental problems: forest destruction and loss of plant and animal life; severe air pollution in São Paulo and nearby industrial towns; soil erosion

continent of South America. (The exceptions are Ecuador and Chile.) In industrial, economic and political terms, Brazil is also the leader of the continent. After having relied heavily on agriculture for many years, Brazil is fast becoming an industrialized nation. This gives Brazil a powerful position among the so-called Third World countries, in their struggle to find equality with the developed nations of the world.

THE LANDSCAPE

Brazil covers nearly half the South American continent, crossed by the equator in the north and the Tropic of Capricorn in the south. From east to west, it covers almost the entire width of the continent, extending from the Atlantic Ocean to within 550 km of the Pacific.

The country is divided into five geographical regions, with 26 states. It includes several small islands. On the mainland, the most northerly region includes the Guiana highlands, formed from ancient rocks and partly forested, where the two highest peaks in Brazil were found as recently as 1953. The Brazilian highlands, a plateau area only 300–900 metres high, broadly cover the centre of the country. To the south-east lies the densely populated coastal strip, mostly just 100 km wide and backed by the steep Great ESCARPMENT, which was once covered with dense rainforest.

The other two regions are the area of the River Amazon to the north, and the TRIBUTARIES that lead to the River Plate system in the south. Together they cover about three-fifths of the country.

In the south many rivers which have their

▼ **Brazil is divided into four time zones. People in Manaus, 1,600 km up the Amazon, are one hour behind their friends in Belém, at the Amazon mouth.**

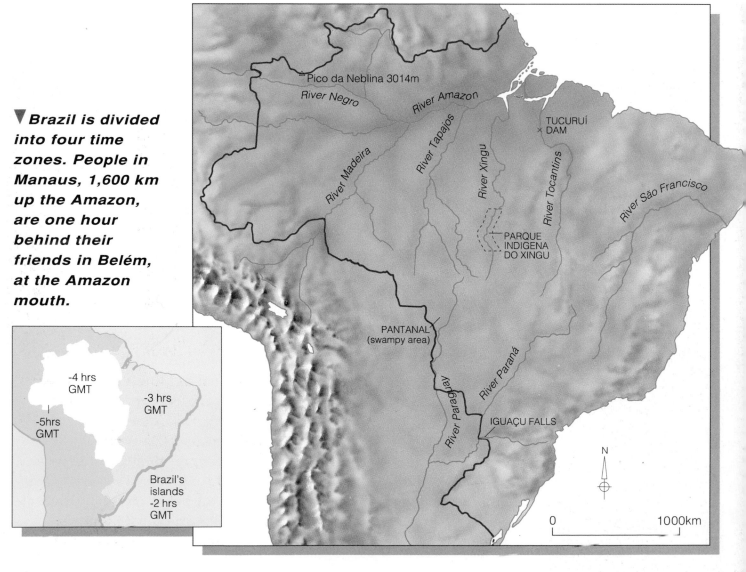

◀ *Much of the north-east is arid savannah, scrub forest, cactus and thorn bushes. Early attempts to raise cattle here failed because it is so dry. It has been called "one of the poorest places on earth".*

KEY FACTS

● Brazil covers 47% of South America.
● Its Atlantic coast-line is 7,369 km long.
● Marajo Island (38,850 sq km) in the Amazon mouth is the world's largest island surrounded by fresh water.
● River São Francisco (2,900 km) is the longest river wholly in Brazil, known as the "river of national unity" as it connects the north-east and south-east.
● River Amazon has 17 tributaries over 1,500 km long. At the sea it discharges water so fast (10 billion litres a second) that fresh water is found 160 km offshore.

▲ *Brazil has many beaches and small natural coves, like this one on the stretch of coast between São Paulo and Rio.*

source in the highlands flow into the River Paraná and the Plate system, following rocky courses with falls and canyons until they reach level ground. The Iguaçu Falls (about 20 metres higher than the Niagara Falls) are on the Iguaçu River, a few kilometres from where it meets the River Paraná. The River Paraguay is another tributary of the Paraná, flowing through an

The Rio Negro, a major Amazon tributary, has its source in the Guiana highlands of northern Brazil. It meets the Amazon near the city of Manaus.

▲ The River Amazon is the world's greatest river and is about 21 times longer than the ◀ River Thames.

▼ Amazonia, the area of South America through which the River Amazon flows, covers 7.5 million sq km. It is almost as large as the USA, as the comparison in this illustration shows.

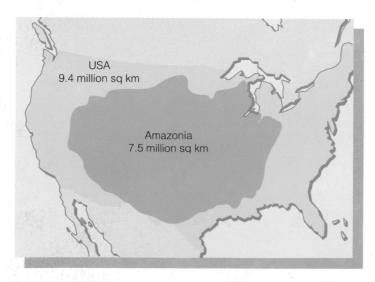

enormous area (140,000 sq km) of level ground called the Pantanal that is a patchwork of lagoons, grassy plains and trees.

Amazonia is the area of 7.5 million sq km in South America where the River Amazon and its 1,000 or more tributaries flow. Almost 5 million sq km of this land is in Brazil and is known to the Brazilians as "Legal Amazonia". It covers approximately 57 per cent of the country and it is not all flat and covered with rainforest. In places it is hilly, even mountainous, and there are regions of grasslands, scrub forests and swamps.

The main Amazon River flows from west to east, mostly within about 400 km south of the equator. The western section of the river in Brazil is known as the Solimões, and only the last 1,500 km to the Atlantic is called Amazon. This great river with its numerous side channels can be as much as 50 km wide, but it narrows to about 2 km at Óbidos, some 1,100 km from the Atlantic Ocean. Then it widens again, forming a mouth 320 km across when it enters the sea.

In the region of Óbidos, rocky hills stand

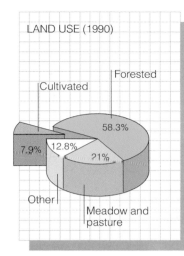

LAND USE (1990)

Cultivated

Forested

58.3%

7.9%

12.8%

21%

Other

Meadow and pasture

Much land in southern Minas Gerais has been cleared of its forests and is used for farming. This road leads to coffee plantations.

above the forest and are part of the very ancient foundation of South America. More of these hills extend across the north-east of Amazonia. The water of the tributaries in this region carries little SEDIMENT and is tea-coloured, due to rotting vegetation.

One Amazon tributary, the Madeira, is more than 3,300 km long: the world's longest tributary. It enters Brazil from Bolivia to the south-west and has a series of gigantic rapids. Another, the Rio Negro, rises in the far north and is over 2,100 km long. Other major rivers flow to the Amazon from the south, many of them rising in higher, grassy lands well beyond the rainforest.

The true rainforest or "moist forest" extends in every direction around the Amazon River and is very varied. Sometimes the trees are giants of 50–60 metres, while others are spindly and only half as tall. Palms are abundant and in some places form extensive forest. Parts of the forest are frequently flooded and the level of the river in the middle section may change by 15 metres or more as rain swells the volume of the tributaries.

The Iguaçu Falls are on the River Iguaçu, close to Brazil's border with Argentina. A total of 275 falls spill over a rocky precipice 60 metres high, at a rate of 1,750 cubic metres a second.

CLIMATE AND WEATHER

Brazil's climate and rainfall can be divided into five zones. Near the equator the temperature hardly changes. Abundant rain, averaging 2,500 mm a year, ensures a luxuriant forest growth that is believed to contain the world's richest BIODIVERSITY.

Immediately north and south of the equatorial zone the climate is tropical. There are two distinct seasons each year, a dry season and a wet season, with an average annual rainfall of about 1,500 mm. The heaviest rains occur in summer (December to February). Both seasons are warm, but with slightly more variation than near the equator. The climate favours grasslands, often with small, rather gnarled trees: this vegetation is known as CERRADO.

▶ *Most of Brazil has a tropical climate. It is cooler only in hilly areas and in the far south, which in winter sometimes has severe frosts.*

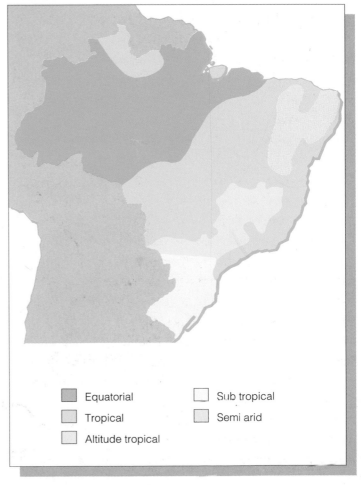

Equatorial

Tropical

Altitude tropical

Sub tropical

Semi arid

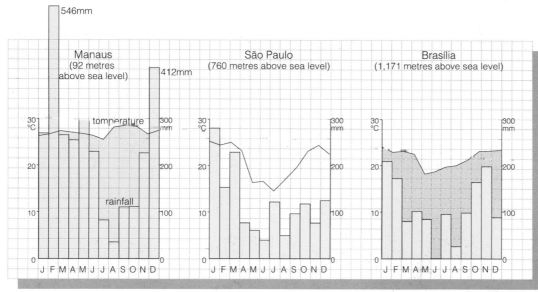

Manaus
(92 metres above sea level)

São Paulo
(760 metres above sea level)

Brasília
(1,171 metres above sea level)

546mm

412mm

temperature

rainfall

◄ *The Amazon city of Manaus, close to the equator, has a hotter climate and is much wetter than either Brasília in the central highlands, or São Paulo near the coast in the south-east.*

◄ *In summer, when temperatures are over 40°C, everyone in Brazil makes for the beaches. Copacabana beach is popular with Brazilians, but tourists prefer Rio's less crowded beaches, like Ipanema.*

The north-east of Brazil is noted for its droughts and harsh climate. Annual rainfall is less than 1,000 mm and the temperature is always high, around 27°C. It is in this region (not the equatorial forests) that the hottest temperatures in Brazil have been recorded. The vegetation is low scrub of sharply spined trees and cacti, called the CAATINGA, where cattle are herded or roam semi-wild.

The southern states are cooler, with a greater range of temperature and distinct seasons. In some winters the frost can damage crops and in the far south of the country snow may settle in mid winter. Heavy tropical storms occasionally strike the coastal region in summer, causing much damage.

Also cooler and subject to frequent winter frosts are tropical highlands, such as the hilly zone to the west of São Paulo and Rio de Janeiro. Here the altitude affects temperatures, which average between 18°C and 22°C, although the difference between low and high can be as much as 7°C–9°C.

▲ *Tropical rain does not last long, but is so heavy that the streets can quickly flood.*

KEY FACTS

● 92% of the country is in the Tropics.
● The poorest part of the north-east, the SERTÃO, is hit by drought every 8 to 15 years and then suffers floods. In 1984 a 5-year drought ended in torrential rains that left 150 dead or missing, and 700,000 homeless.

NATURAL RESOURCES

Brazil is immensely rich in natural resources, particularly in the states of Pará, Minas Gerais and Rondônia. It was in Minas Gerais that the early explorers, the BANDEIRANTES, first discovered gold in 1693. Brazil's first gold rush followed this. There have been others since, one of the most recent in Serra Pelada in the Amazon.

Carajás, thought to be the world's largest iron deposit, was discovered in 1967. Today, Brazil is estimated to have a third of the world's iron ore reserves, the basis of its steel industry.

Other minerals in Brazil include coal, bauxite, manganese, zinc, nickel, lead, cobalt, cadmium, copper, chrome and tin. There are reserves of gypsum, titanium, phosphates and platinum too. Deposits of nobium, thought to be the world's largest, have been found in Amazonas. Brazil also supplies 90 per cent of the world market for several semi-precious gems, including amethyst and topaz.

Energy resources include large deposits of oil off the coast and in the states of Rio Grande do Norte, Sergipe, Bahia and Ceará, and big gas reserves. Above all there are thousands of kilometres of rivers, with potential for hydro-electricity, and dams are being built for this. The Itaipú Dam on the River Paraná achieved the world's greatest output of hydro-electric power when the second stage was completed in 1990.

The country's timber reserves are reckoned to be the world's third largest. Most of the wood is used as fuel, but

▶ *When gold was found in 1980 on Serra Pelada in Amazonia, within a month more than 10,000 gold prospectors rushed to the area.*

▼ *Carajás has the world's largest known iron-ore deposit. It also contains bauxite, manganese and copper.*

softwoods, particularly parana pine and eucalyptus, are grown in the south for local pulp and paper industries. Hardwoods from the rainforest include mahogany, which is much favoured for furniture by countries like the UK and USA. The felling and export of hardwoods has become very controversial and has caused considerable damage to the rainforests.

KEY FACTS

● The world's largest topaz and emerald have both been found in Brazil.
● Brazil took its name from the Brazilwood tree, from which 16th century Portuguese settlers extracted a dye. It is one of 400 hardwoods found in the forests.
● 75% of Brazil's oil reserves are offshore.
● In the late 1800s, latex from the Amazon tree *Hevea brasiliensis* was in huge demand for rubber goods. But the Amazon lost out after the tree began to be grown in Asia.

◈ POPULATION

THE ORIGINAL PEOPLES

The native peoples of Brazil lived in the forests and along the rivers, hunting, fishing, and gathering fruits and nuts. When the Portuguese arrived early in the 16th century, it is estimated that there were between 1 and 2 million native people. Europeans called them Indians. They were used as slaves and many thousands died from diseases brought by the Europeans. Recently they have been killed as land speculators and highways go further into the rainforest. There are probably less than 150,000 Indians now.

Although the Statute of the Indian Law of 1978 was meant to define Indian lands, many COLONISTS and ranchers ignore this. Some reserves, such as Xingu Park, have been created, but increasingly Indian

▲ *This crowd of people watching Carnival in Rio is made up of some of the different peoples that form Brazilian society. There are mestiços, whites, blacks and mulattos.*

◀ *A Kayapo Indian family. The Indian way of life is changing (see the father's watch), but some traditional customs remain.*

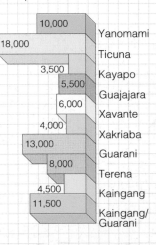

POPULATIONS (approx) OF THE BETTER KNOWN TRIBES (1985)

Population	Tribe
10,000	Yanomami
18,000	Ticuna
3,500	Kayapo
5,500	Guajajara
6,000	Xavante
4,000	Xakriaba
13,000	Guarani
8,000	Terena
4,500	Kaingang
11,500	Kaingang/Guarani

RACIAL MIX (1989)

Indians and Asians 0.5%
Whites 55.8%
Mixed races 36.8%
Blacks 4.8%

◀ **This diagram shows the different groups that make up Brazil's population.**

▼ **These two maps show how in 50 years, as the population has increased, people have moved near the coast, where the major cities are found.**

people are taking matters into their own hands, even using arms to defend themselves.

BLACKS, MULATTOS AND MESTIÇOS

Portuguese settlers developed vast sugar cane estates in the Bahia region, and for 150 years these were the world's main source of sugar. To work the estates, the owners used slaves from Africa. Today there is still an African tradition in Brazil.

During the 400 years of Portuguese rule, marriages between Europeans and Indians, and Europeans and Africans, produced two new groups: the olive-skinned MESTIÇOS and the darker MULATTOS.

KEY FACTS

● The people of Rio are known as "Cariocas".
● Brazil's fastest growing city is São Paulo. Its population was 6 million in the late 1960s; today it is about 10 million.
● São Paulo has the world's largest Japanese community outside Japan.
● FUNAI is the state organization created in 1968 to protect the rights of the Indian peoples in Brazil.

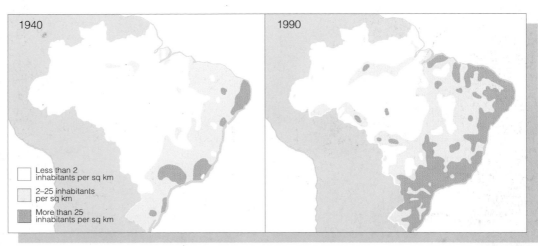

1940

1990

Less than 2 inhabitants per sq km

2–25 inhabitants per sq km

More than 25 inhabitants per sq km

IMMIGRANTS

Modern immigration began early in the 19th century. Only about 4.5 million foreigners, mostly from Europe, settled in Brazil after then. Most were Italians and Portuguese, but there were also Spanish and Germans, and later Slavs from Poland, Russia and the Ukraine, and Arabs from the Middle East. The Germans in particular, and some Italians, set up farms in the southern states of Santa Catarina, Rio Grande do Sul and Paraná.

In this century the most significant immigrants have been Japanese, who have become the most prosperous ethnic group in Brazil, growing a fifth of the coffee, a third of the cotton and all the tea.

INTERNAL MIGRATION

Traditionally the majority of Brazilians settled near the coast, but in the last 30 years the rapid movement from rural areas to urban centres has led to a very uneven distribution of the population. In parts of the interior there is an average of just one person per square kilometre. Over 75 per cent of the people live in towns; half of these are in just two cities: São Paulo and Rio de Janeiro.

People have moved from rural areas to the towns to seek work and better medical and educational facilities for their families. But the reality has been very different. Tens of thousands of people now live in shanty towns, or FAVELAS, on the outskirts of the cities, with little hope of ever getting a real job.

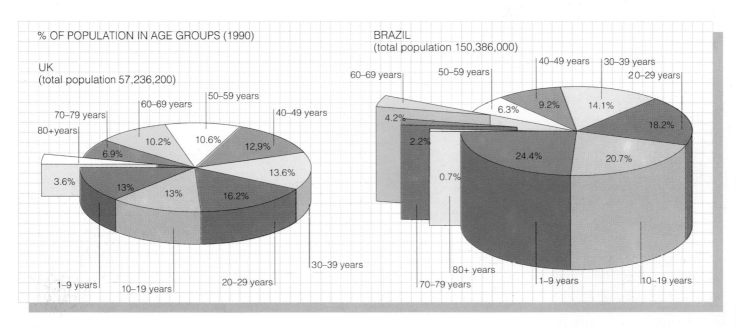

% OF POPULATION IN AGE GROUPS (1990)

UK (total population 57,236,200)

- 70–79 years
- 80+ years
- 60–69 years
- 50–59 years
- 40–49 years
- 10.2%
- 10.6%
- 12.9%
- 6.9%
- 13.6%
- 3.6%
- 13%
- 13%
- 16.2%
- 1–9 years
- 10–19 years
- 20–29 years
- 30–39 years

BRAZIL (total population 150,386,000)

- 60–69 years
- 50–59 years
- 40–49 years
- 30–39 years
- 20–29 years
- 4.2%
- 6.3%
- 9.2%
- 14.1%
- 18.2%
- 2.2%
- 24.4%
- 20.7%
- 0.7%
- 80+ years
- 70–79 years
- 1–9 years
- 10–19 years

◄ *A skyline of highrises in downtown São Paulo, Brazil's largest and fastest growing city. Founded in 1554, its population 100 years ago was 31,000, but then coffee planters began to move in. Today it has around 10 million people, with some 17 million in metropolitan São Paulo.*

▶ *The African tradition in Brazil is especially strong around the city of Salvador in Bahia, with colourful dress, rhythmic music and exotic food all part of this culture. Here a Bahiana woman in traditional dress sells typical African-style snacks of "aracajes", a bean dumpling fried in palm oil and mixed with dried shrimp and coconut milk paté.*

DAILY LIFE

◀ *In the slums, or "favelas", of Rio de Janeiro, home is often just one room.*

HEALTH STATISTICS	Brazil	USA	China	UK
Population estimate for 2025 (millions)	245.8	299.9	1,512.6	59.7
Urban growth, 1990–5 (%)	2.7	0.9	5.4	0.3
% urban 1990	75	75	33	89
Life expectancy in 1990 (years)	66	76	71	76
Death rate per 1,000	7	9	7	11
Birth rate per 1,000	26	14	21	14

▼ *About a quarter of the population of Rio de Janeiro live in favelas. Conditions are very poor and often there is no water, light or sanitation.*

FAMILY LIFE

Family ties are strong in Brazil. Three generations, including grandparents and young married couples, often live together in one house. Poorer families are frequently large, with five or six children, and grandparents look after the very young while the rest of the family work.

There is a wide gap between rich and poor. The wealthy live in luxury mansions or on vast estates, employ maids and gardeners, and enjoy the same consumer goods as any family in the developed world. Homes for the poor are shacks of cardboard and corrugated iron, furnished with the barest essentials and mostly without water, light or sanitation.

EDUCATION

Attendance at primary school (age 7–14) is compulsory and free in state schools. There are also private, fee-paying and Church-run schools. However, some 2 million children do not attend school – many because they have no school to go to. Less than a fifth of

KEY FACTS

● Footballer Edson Arantes do Nascimento (Pelé) has scored the most goals ever in a specified time: 1,363 between 7 September 1956 and 1 October 1977.

● Brazil has over 20,000 football teams.

● Divorce was only legalized in 1977.

● In Brazil there are over 2,500 radio stations and 6 TV networks, of which TV Globo is the largest. There are no national newspapers because distribution throughout Brazil is too expensive. Most cities have their own newspapers.

● In 1990 there were 95 universities, of which 55 were run by the state.

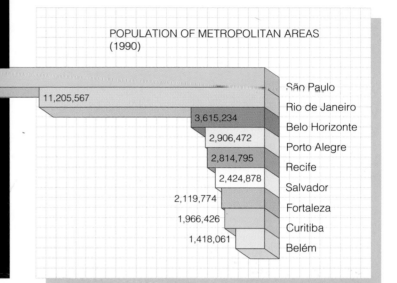

POPULATION OF METROPOLITAN AREAS (1990)

17,112,712	São Paulo
11,205,567	Rio de Janeiro
3,615,234	Belo Horizonte
2,906,472	Porto Alegre
2,814,795	Recife
2,424,878	Salvador
2,119,774	Fortaleza
1,966,426	Curitiba
1,418,061	Belém

all students go on to secondary school (age 15–18) and only a tiny percentage enter university. Most schools are in urban areas, and these have better equipment and facilities than schools in rural regions.

Almost 20 per cent of the population cannot read or write. This includes people who live in very remote areas or belong to Indian tribes. Indian peoples have their own languages and often know little Portuguese, the official language of Brazil.

SOCIAL PROBLEMS

The extreme poverty in the urban slums, the high unemployment and the increasing numbers leaving rural areas for the cities have led to serious social problems.

The poorest people suffer most as the state cannot provide for them, but children who live and work in the streets, trying to

▶ *Instead of going to school, many children work to earn money for their families. This young boy is helping to sort and pack fish for the market in Manaus.*

▲One of Brasília's most spectacular buildings is the circular cathedral, in the shape of a crown of thorns and surrounded by a moat. The interior (shown here) is below ground level.

▶Many Brazilians make pilgrimages to the statue of Padre Cicero from Ceará, who died in 1934. Local people regard him as a saint.

MAIN NATIONAL HOLIDAYS

1 January	NEW YEAR'S DAY
Feb/March	CARNIVAL AND GOOD FRIDAY
March/April	EASTER
21 April	TIRADENTES DAY
1 May	LABOUR DAY
May/June	CORPUS CHRISTI
7 September	INDEPENDENCE DAY
12 October	PATRONESS SAINT OF BRAZIL
15 November	PROCLAMATION OF THE REPUBLIC
25 December	CHRISTMAS

earn extra income for their families, are particularly at risk. They may get involved in theft and robbery, which is commonplace in many cities, and also in more serious crimes such as drug abuse. Brazil has a high murder rate, and many children have been victims of street violence.

LEISURE

Football is the favourite sport for most Brazilians. Rio's Maracana stadium is the largest in the world. Brazilians also make the most of their beaches, relaxing in the sun, playing ball games or water-sports and following keep-fit routines.

The greatest yearly event in Brazil is Carnival, which takes place in February or March. In Rio de Janeiro thousands of people, rich and poor, take part. They dance in the streets, wearing glittering costumes which take months to prepare.

▲ *The Brazilian football team that defeated Sweden 2–1 in the World Cup held in Italy in 1990. Brazil is the only country to have played in all 15 World Cup tournaments.*

RELIGION

Some 90 per cent of Brazil's population belong to the Roman Catholic Church. Other religions include the Protestant Church, the Baha'i faith and Buddhism.

The people of African descent still follow the religions of their ancestors. The main cults are Candomblé, Macumba and Umbanda. Priests and priestesses lead members in lively celebration of their gods, with frenzied sessions of songs and dances accompanied by beating drums.

The Indian peoples celebrate their own gods and spirits with music, song and dance.

RULE AND LAW

Brazil became an independent country in 1822 when Dom Pedro I was crowned Emperor. His son, Dom Pedro II, introduced many reforms. When he passed the "Golden Law" to abolish slavery, this angered the wealthy landowners; they plotted with the military to depose him, and the empire ended.

Since 1889, when Brazil became a republic, there have been both military and civilian governments. One successful President was Getúlio Vargas (1930–1945 and 1950–1954), known as the "Father of the Poor" because of the measures he took to try and improve the welfare of the people. Another President, Juscelino Kubitschek, in 1960 founded the new capital city, Brasília, on an uninhabited plateau in central Brazil.

From 1964 till 1985, there was a military government, with political repression and torture of its opponents, but also economic success. The military eventually agreed to a new electoral college, which in 1985 voted in the first civilian President for 21 years. The Constitution was revised to ensure that five years later the next President was elected by the people. All persons aged 18 to 69 who are literate must vote; those who are illiterate, aged over 70, or between 16 and 17 years old may do so if they wish.

Two years after taking office, in 1992 the new President, Fernando Collor, was forced to resign on corruption charges and was replaced by the Vice-President. Collor's fall shocked Brazilians.

Brasília is now home to the Congress building, ministries, President's office and

▼ *In 1985 a civilian president was elected by an electoral college. By 1990 direct elections, with everyone able to vote, had been restored.*

KEY FACTS

● Brazil has had 3 capital cities: first Salvador de Bahia, (till 1763), then Rio de Janeiro (till 1960) and now Brasília.

● Brazil was the last western country to abolish slavery, in 1888; some 700,000 slaves were freed.

● Women were granted the vote in 1934.

● A year's military service is compulsory for all men aged 18.

● In 1982 Mario Juruna was the first Indian to be elected as a Senator.

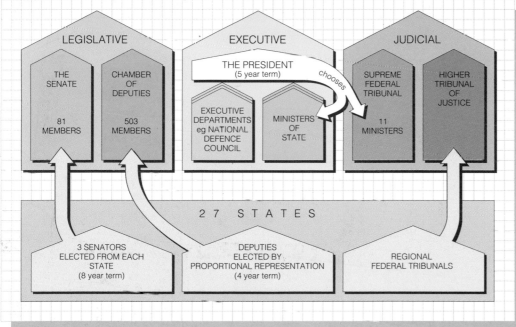

LEGISLATIVE		EXECUTIVE		JUDICIAL	
THE SENATE	CHAMBER OF DEPUTIES	THE PRESIDENT (5 year term) *chooses*		SUPREME FEDERAL TRIBUNAL	HIGHER TRIBUNAL OF JUSTICE
81 MEMBERS	503 MEMBERS	EXECUTIVE DEPARTMENTS eg NATIONAL DEFENCE COUNCIL	MINISTERS OF STATE	11 MINISTERS	

27 STATES

3 SENATORS ELECTED FROM EACH STATE (8 year term)	DEPUTIES ELECTED BY PROPORTIONAL REPRESENTATION (4 year term)	REGIONAL FEDERAL TRIBUNALS

▲ **The Congress building in Brasília is where the Chamber of Deputies and the Senate sit. It was designed by Oscar Niemeyer, Brazil's leading architect.**

▼ **Brazil's police force have to deal with a high level of theft and robbery.**

more than a million people. Congress is made up of the Chamber of Deputies and the Senate, who make the laws by which the country is governed. They are also responsible for financial policy and relations with other countries. The President needs approval from Congress for many acts, but he can veto laws passed by them. The 26 states and the Federal District elect their own governor and legislature, and each state is divided into MUNICIPIOS, each of which elects a mayor.

▲ **Brazil is governed by the President, Federal Senate and Chamber of Deputies. The President and Senators must be at least 35 years old, and Deputies 21 years old.**

FOOD AND FARMING

Sugar, introduced in the 16th century by the Portuguese, was the first commercially successful agricultural crop in Brazil, followed early in the 18th century by coffee, brought in from French Guiana. Coffee grew well on the hilly uplands west of Rio de Janeiro and São Paulo, and in the southern states, where it has been concentrated since, though some is grown in the Amazon region too. Today, Brazil is the world's largest producer and exporter of both sugar and coffee.

The south is Brazil's richest agricultural area. But farming lacks the advanced technology widely used in the USA.

Throughout Brazil, only 20 per cent of arable land is cultivated and the agricultural industry employs less than a quarter of the working population.

Yet Brazil is almost self-sufficient in food production, except for wheat, and agricultural production accounts for about a third of exports. As well as coffee and sugar, major crops are soya, cocoa, cotton, tobacco and maize. Rice, sorghum and beans are grown for the domestic market. All kinds of fruits are plentiful, with some like "maracuja" or passion fruit now familiar in western markets. Currently Brazil supplies 85 per cent of the world market for orange juice concentrates. The forests also provide a range of nuts, of which the Brazil nut is the best known.

Although about a quarter of Brazilians live in the countryside, very few own their land. It is a major problem that 80 per cent of land is owned by just 5 per cent of the population, and this has led to considerable violence between would-be settlers and gunmen ("pistoleiros") hired by landowners. Opening up the Amazon forest has not proved to be the solution either. Colonists who received grants of land from the government have found it difficult to make the small farms pay, and many have been forced to sell out to wealthy landowners or speculators. In addition, between 1985 and 1989, 350 people in the Amazonas were killed by pistoleiros. Ranching has met with little more success, again because the land is poor. In some places, 25 hectares are needed to support just one cow.

The main centre of Brazil's cattle industry, which overall contributes some 10 per cent to world trade, is in the south and to a lesser extent in the north-east. Cowboys known as GAUCHOS herd the

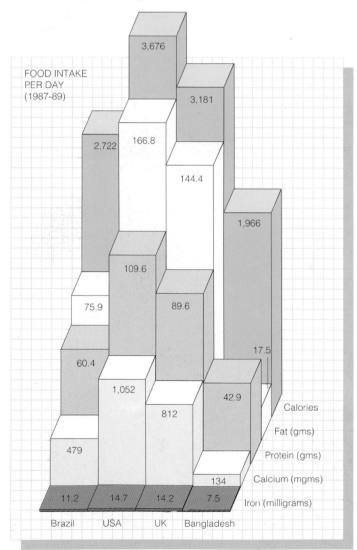

FOOD INTAKE PER DAY (1987-89)

	Brazil	USA	UK	Bangladesh
Calories	2,722	3,676	3,181	1,966
Fat (gms)	75.9	166.8	144.4	42.9
Protein (gms)	60.4	109.6	89.6	17.5
Calcium (mgms)	479	1,052	812	134
Iron (milligrams)	11.2	14.7	14.2	7.5

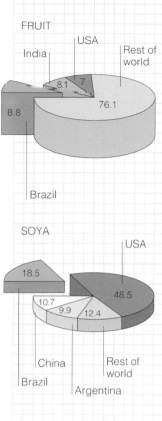

% OF WORLD MARKETS (1990)
(depth = total production)

FRUIT

India | USA | Rest of world
8.1 | 7 | 76.1
8.8
Brazil

SOYA

USA
18.5 | 48.5
10.7
9.9 | 12.4
China | Rest of world
Brazil | Argentina

SUGAR

India | Cuba
25.5 | 21.2 | 7.4
39.7 | 6.2
Brazil | Rest of world | China

COFFEE

Colombia | Indonesia
Mexico
24.2 | 13.4 | 6.5 | 5.2
50.7
Brazil | Rest of world

Brazil is a major world producer of fruit and much of this is for export. But local market stalls are always well stocked with fresh produce. Fruit in Brazil is cheap.

The coffee picking season in Minas Gerais is from May to July. The coffee beans are then dried, sorted, washed and bagged before being transported to the docks at Santos, ready for export.

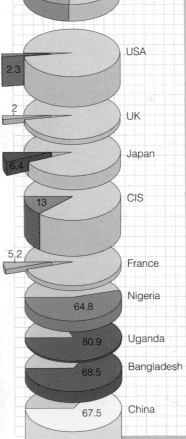

KEY FACTS

● The largest Amazon catfish, the piraiba, can grow to more than 3 metres long and 1.5 metres around the body, weighing about 200 kilos.
● The world's largest shrimp bank is found in the mouth of the Amazon.
● 75% of all Brazilian wine comes from the southern state of Rio Grande do Sul.
● Between November 1991 and October 1992 Brazil exported 20,349,000 sacks of coffee, each holding 60 kilos.
● Brazil is a leading world producer of tobacco, and more than three-quarters of the crop is grown in the State of Bahia.

% OF PEOPLE EMPLOYED IN AGRICULTURE (1990)
(depth = work force)

24.3	Brazil
2.3	USA
2	UK
6.4	Japan
13	CIS
5.2	France
64.8	Nigeria
80.9	Uganda
68.5	Bangladesh
67.5	China

▲ *Cowboys in Brazil leading a herd of zebu cattle, raised for the beef industry. As a breed they survive well in dry and harsh areas.*

▶ *A small area of tropical forest remains here in southern Brazil. The remaining forest has been cleared to make way for cultivation. Contour farming follows the line of the low hills.*

millions of cattle that roam the vast grasslands of the south. They wear flat black hats and baggy trousers called "bombachas". Their favourite drink is a herbal tea, or "mate". In contrast, the cowboys of the north-east, the VAQUEIROS, wear leather hats and trousers to protect their legs from the spiny scrub and cacti of the arid caatingas.

Although it has the longest continuous coastline in the world, Brazil has only a small fishing industry. Much of the catch is for the home market and it is caught by local village fishermen. Off the north-east coast fishermen use boats called JANGADAS, which traditionally were made of logs lashed together. Today most are manufactured from plastic tubing.

Food in Brazil varies according to the region. In cattle country in the south, huge quantities of meat are always available, while in the north-east the African-style Bahian dishes are mostly based on fish. Shrimps, crab meat or white fish, mixed with coconut milk, "dende" oil from a palm, nuts and spices, and served with rice, manioc or corn meal, make a truly exotic dish.

The national dish of Brazil is FEIJOADA. This meal is traditionally eaten on Saturdays and lasts for many hours. It is made of black beans, various types of dried and smoked meats – these can include ordinary cuts of pork or beef, but also pigs' feet and beef tongues – fried manioc flour and rice. Other side dishes include fresh oranges and dried kale.

TRADE AND INDUSTRY

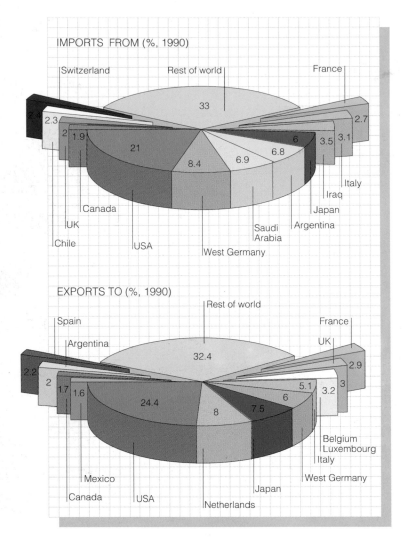

IMPORTS FROM (%, 1990)

Switzerland · Rest of world · France
33
2.3 · 2.7
2 · 1.9 · 6 · 3.5 · 3.1
21 · 6.8
8.4 · 6.9
Canada · Italy
UK · Iraq
Chile · Japan
USA · Saudi Arabia · Argentina
West Germany

EXPORTS TO (%, 1990)

Spain · Rest of world · France
Argentina · UK
32.4
2.2 · 2.9
2 · 3
1.7 · 1.6 · 5.1 · 3.2
24.4 · 6
8 · 7.5
Mexico · Belgium Luxembourg
Canada · Italy
USA · West Germany
Netherlands · Japan

DEBT AND INFLATION

Since the Second World War, industry has taken over from agriculture as the basis of Brazil's economy. Billions of dollars have been spent in achieving this, first in the 1950s and then in the 1970s when the "Brazilian miracle" took place that transformed Brazil into an industrial nation. The generals who were in charge in the 1970s borrowed vast sums from international banks, which paid for the "miracle" but left the country big debts. Today Brazil has the largest foreign debt of any country in the world. Repaying it is an almost impossible task for a developing nation, even though Brazil in recent years has seen its exports exceeding imports.

Brazil has also suffered from high inflation, with prices of food and other goods increasing almost daily. Between 1986 and 1990 the currency was altered three times: in 1986 1,000 cruzeiros was reduced to equal 1 cruzado, in 1989 the cruzado was replaced by the new cruzado and in 1990 the new cruzado was replaced

▲ *Brazil trades more with the USA than with any other country.*

▶ *Mahogany felled in the south of Pará state is cut and stacked ready for export from Belém, at the mouth of the Amazon.*

The Itaipú Dam was begun in 1975 and began generating electricity in 1984. It is 624 feet (190 m) high, its walls are 542 feet (165 m) thick, and a lake was formed behind the dam that covers 118 miles (190 km).

KEY FACTS

● In 1990 about 1 million tourists visited Brazil.

● The country's international debt in 1992 was estimated at $125 billion.

● Brazil's major ports are Santos (São Paulo), Rio de Janeiro, Paranaguá, Recife, and Vitória. Santos and Rio handle about half of all cargo.

● Brazil makes more than 1 million cars every year.

● With the creation of Itaipú Dam on the Paraná River for hydroelectric power, Sete Quedas, the world's largest waterfall (in volume) disappeared.

HYDRO-ELECTRICITY (1991)
Comparison of size of output from dams in the world (megawatts)

12,600	Itaipú, Brazil
10,300	Gurí, Venezuela
9,700	Grand Coulee, USA
6,400	Sayano-Shushenek, CIS
3,960	Tucuruí, Brazil
130	Lock Sloy, UK

by the cruzeiro. With each change the value of Brazilian money has declined. In 1994 the currency changed to the New real.

MANUFACTURING INDUSTRY

One aspect of the "Brazilian miracle" was the development of manufacturing industries. State-run companies were established to run important industries, such as oil, steel, communications, and electricity. Foreign companies were invited to set up in the country, and large-scale industries were established for the construction of ships, vehicles of every kind, and aircraft. The vast majority of consumer items used in Brazil, such as washing machines, refrigerators, televisions, and other household goods, are now manufactured there.

Technologically-based industries also developed, with demand for electronic and computer equipment, but traditional

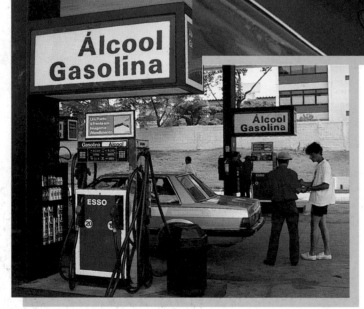

▼ *Alcohol distilled from sugar cane is sold from pumps alongside petrol in most fuel stations. The majority of cars made in Brazil are adapted to use "alcool".*

▲ *Of all the cars made in Brazil, the VW "beetle" was for many years the most popular. In cities it was used as a taxi. It was also suitable for rough rural roads.*

products such as textiles, clothing and processed food and drink are still important. Most shoe-shops in Britain, for example, sell a range of Brazilian-made shoes, while Brazilian aircraft are used commercially in Britain and to train members of its air force. Timber has become more important, with softwoods used locally for paper and hardwoods being felled for export.

Industry now accounts for about 70 per cent of total exports and employs about a quarter of Brazil's work force. Most industry is heavily concentrated in the south-east, around the cities of São Paulo, Rio and Belo Horizonte.

MINERALS AND MINING

Brazil is now beginning to realize the potential of its immensely rich mineral resources. International banks and organizations have helped to develop the Grande Carajás iron-ore mine, and to build a new 890-km long railway through the forest to a specially constructed new port near São Luis.

Brazil is a major exporter and producer not only of iron, but also of bauxite, from which aluminium is extracted, and in 1991 it was the world's leading producer of

34

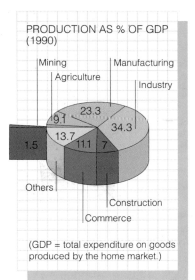

PRODUCTION AS % OF GDP (1990)

Mining
Agriculture
Manufacturing
Industry

9.1
23.3
34.3
13.7
11.1 7
1.5

Others

Construction
Commerce

(GDP = total expenditure on goods produced by the home market.)

◄ *Brazil's economy used to be based on agriculture. This chart shows how Industry and manufacturing goods have overtaken agriculture and now represent almost 60% of the nation's output.*

over 90 per cent of the nation's electricity. The Itaipú Dam, built jointly by Brazil and Paraguay on the River Paraná, is now in its second stage. Its output of 12,600 megawatts is the largest in the world. Other such large projects include Tucuruí in the Amazon, and a proposed dam on the Xingu River that is planned to have an output of 17,000 megawatts.

In an attempt to reduce the expensive import of oil, in the 1970s and 1980s the government sponsored a programme to use sugar cane alcohol as the basis of a new fuel, "alcool". This was very successful – of all cars sold in Brazil in 1984, 85 per cent were alcohol-powered. As the price of imported oil has dropped, this programme has been cut back and Brazil has begun to develop its own oil reserves. It is now the third largest oil producer in Latin America and by 1993 expects to be totally self-sufficient.

cassiterite, the mineral from which tin is made. There are also substantial gold reserves in the Amazon region.

ENERGY

The potential for hydro-electric power in Brazil is enormous, and it already provides

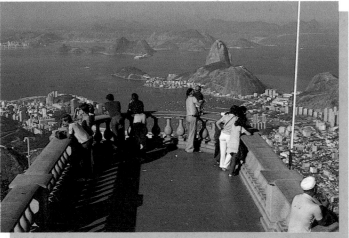

◄ ▲ *Two of Rio de Janeiro's best known landmarks are the statue of Christ on Corcovado (Hunchback) Mountain, and the Sugar Loaf Mountain at the entrance to Guanabara Bay. The statue is 40 metres high, weighs 1,145 tonnes and was completed in 1931.*

TRANSPORT

For centuries the most reliable way of travelling in Brazil was by river. Most freight and passengers now go by road or air, but rivers are still an important communication link in some remote areas, and ocean-going ships still travel to Manaus, 1,600 km up the Amazon. Santos, 63 km from São Paulo, is now the busiest of Brazil's ports, handling 30 per cent of all cargo.

Some railways were introduced in the 19th century, mainly connected with mines, but in the country as a whole there are few railways for general passenger travel.

A dramatic increase in road building over the last 30 years has now linked Brasília, in the heart of the country, to most outlying areas. The first of the Amazon highways connected Brasília to Belém at the mouth of the Amazon River, while the most recent links the west of the Amazon to the industrial south-east, providing a route along which much of the newly felled timber is carried to the coast. The most ambitious current project is the 5,000 km Trans-Amazonian Highway from Recife in the north-east to the Peruvian border. Roads now carry 60 per cent of the country's freight and 95 per cent of passenger traffic, much of them on Brazil's excellent long-distance bus service.

The greatest problem in Brazil is its sheer size. Air transport has transformed

KEY FACTS

● There are 43,000 kilometres of navigable rivers in Brazil.
● VARIG, Brazil's major airline, is the largest in Latin America.
● Both Rio de Janeiro and São Paulo have metro (underground railway) systems. They each consist of two lines and operate every day except Sundays.

▼ *The floating dock in Manaus harbour was designed in 1902 to cope with the annual rise and fall in the river's water levels. It is connected to street level by a floating ramp.*

► **VARIG is the largest Brazilian airline. The other main companies are Transbrasil, VASP and Cruzeiro do Sul. Together in 1990 they transported some 17,049,000 passengers.**

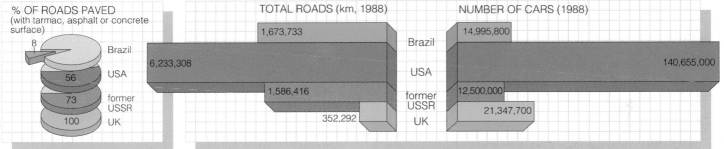

% OF ROADS PAVED (with tarmac, asphalt or concrete surface)		TOTAL ROADS (km, 1988)		NUMBER OF CARS (1988)	
8	Brazil	1,673,733	Brazil	14,995,800	Brazil
56	USA	6,233,308	USA	140,655,000	USA
73	former USSR	1,586,416	former USSR	12,500,000	former USSR
100	UK	352,292	UK	21,347,700	UK

► *Part of the Trans-Amazon Highway, cut through the Amazon rainforest. Highways in Amazonia are expensive to build and to maintain. Many are not paved and can be very difficult to travel in the rainy season.*

communication over very long distances. There are regular services on major routes between main cities, and frequent flights to remote, outlying regions where small planes can land on grass landing strips, or if necessary amphibian planes alight on the rivers. But for many people, flying is an expensive way to travel.

Older forms of transport, such as horses and carts, are still much in use in rural areas. Water buffalo and carts are used in Marajó Island. However, many more people are taking to bicycles and, if they can afford them, to motorbikes which can cope with dirt roads and are fast.

THE RAINFOREST

Brazil has over a quarter of the world's rainforest and about a tenth of all known plant and animal species. Scientists admit that they still have much to learn about the Amazon rainforest. Several of the animals there, such as the tapir, capybara and many species of monkey, exist only in Central and South American forests. Even now, previously unknown mammals are still being discovered and the botanical finds seem limitless.

"Legal Amazonia" covers almost 60 per cent of Brazil. Yet in 1960 only about 2 million people lived there, out of a total population of over 70 million. In the 1960s thousands of people in Brazil moved from rural areas in the north-east and from the south to live in overcrowded city slums. So

▲In February 1989 the Kayapo Indians organized a meeting at Altamira to protest against planned development in the Amazon. Indians from all over Brazil met together there.

▶The Brazilian government estimates that the rate of destruction of the rainforest in Legal Amazonia has fallen from 21,500 sq km in 1978/88 to 13,818 sq km in 1989/90.

many people needing homes and facilities put great pressure on cities like São Paulo and Rio de Janeiro, and to move them to the Amazon region seemed an obvious solution. Since then governments have looked to the region for an answer to some of Brazil's social and economic problems. By doing so, they have opened up the area

DISTRIBUTION OF THE WORLD'S RAINFOREST (1989) (%)

Brazil | Others
27.5 | 23
49.5

Burma, Colombia, India, Indonesia, Malaysia, Mexico, Nigeria, Thailand, Zaire

RATES OF DEFORESTATION (1990)

2.3%

Brazil

Indonesia
1.4%

Burma
3.3%

Mexico
4.2%

Colombia
2.3%

Thailand
8.4%

Malaysia
3.1%

Nigeria
14.3%

India
2.4%

Zaire
0.4%

(Depth shows relative size of forest areas that have been destroyed)

▼ *The Hyacinth Macaw is one of many Amazon birds on the endangered list, which also includes the jaguar. Several species are already extinct.*

to settlers carrying chainsaws, shotguns and rubbish.

DESTRUCTION OF THE FOREST

Cutting highways through the forest was the first stage of the operation. Then people were offered money and land to settle there, but they soon realized that the land was not as fertile as it seemed. Almost all the forest's richness is in the trees. When they are cut down and burned, the valuable ash left behind is a good fertilizer for a few years but is soon washed away by the tropical rain. Any bare ground quickly hardens or is eroded by water and becomes unusable.

Commercial interests have also been responsible for destroying large areas of the forest. Although the Carajás iron-ore project has created little disturbance at the mine itself, much damage has occurred as people have settled along the railway line. Some Indians have had to move from their land. A further threat to the environment has come from small-scale iron-ore smelters around the mine which are fuelled

by charcoal made from wood cut from the forest at a rate of more than 1,000 sq km a year. The nearby Tucuruí Dam and other hydro-electric projects have led to further destruction.

The discovery of new gold deposits in the Amazon has led to thousands of gold-diggers, or "garimpeiros", invading the sites. They damage the rainforest, pollute the rivers with the mercury that they use to separate the gold from the earth, and threaten the existence of Indian tribes who stand in their way. The situation of the Yanomani Indians is perhaps the most tragic, as the discovery of diamonds, tin and gold on their territory has led to them losing a third of their land.

The newest threat to the forest is the growing timber industry. In their search for mahogany and other hardwoods, loggers often destroy many hectares of other trees.

Estimates of the extent of damage to the rainforest vary greatly, but in Brazil's "Legal Amazonia" 8.5 per cent (415,000 sq km) have so far been cleared. However, recent satellite photographs show that since the

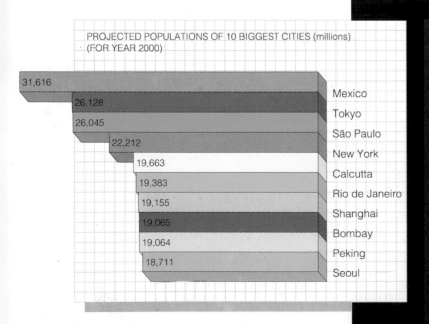

PROJECTED POPULATIONS OF 10 BIGGEST CITIES (millions) (FOR YEAR 2000)

31,616	Mexico
26,128	Tokyo
26,045	São Paulo
22,212	New York
19,663	Calcutta
19,383	Rio de Janeiro
19,155	Shanghai
19,065	Bombay
19,064	Peking
18,711	Seoul

KEY FACTS

● The Amazon is thought to contain about 3,000 species of fish.

● At the end of 1992 two cities in the Amazon, Belém and Manaus, each had a population of over 1 million.

● The first European expedition to explore the length of the Amazon was in 1541–2.

● Scientists estimate that a patch of typical rainforest of 6 sq km contains different species of 1,500 flowering plants, 750 trees, 400 birds, 150 butterflies, 100 reptiles and 60 amphibians. Insects are too many to be counted.

▲Cubatão, between Santos and São Paulo, was one of the world's most polluted places. In 1984 a petrol pipeline laid across a swamp leaked and 90 people died when their homes caught fire. Since then the industries have invested in pollution control.

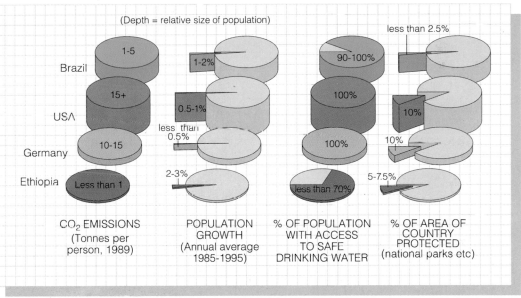

(Depth = relative size of population)

	CO₂ EMISSIONS (Tonnes per person, 1989)	POPULATION GROWTH (Annual average 1985-1995)	% OF POPULATION WITH ACCESS TO SAFE DRINKING WATER	% OF AREA OF COUNTRY PROTECTED (national parks etc)
Brazil	1-5	1-2%	90-100%	less than 2.5%
USA	15+	0.5-1%	100%	10%
Germany	10-15	less than 0.5%	100%	10%
Ethiopia	Less than 1	2-3%	less than 70%	5-7.5%

late 1980s destruction of the Amazon forest in Brazil has been much reduced.

THE GREENHOUSE EFFECT

Many people are concerned that burning the forest contributes to global warming, or the "Greenhouse Effect", which is changing weather patterns. One reason for this warmth may be increased carbon dioxide and other gases in the atmosphere.

However, burning Amazon forest added less than 2 per cent to the world's carbon dioxide in 1991, while pollution from cars and industry in the USA added more than 22 per cent. So the danger of global warming from the Amazon fires is relatively small. Concern is now turning more to the continuing loss of the Amazon rainforest and its great variety of unique animal and plant species.

THE FUTURE

In 1992 Brazil was host to the Rio 92 Earth Summit Conference, attended by more than 100 heads of state. The agenda included a plan to limit carbon dioxide emissions and a proposal to preserve the world's great biodiversity, which was agreed by almost every country except the USA.

Brazil has already recognized its special place in the environment and has taken measures to reduce rainforest destruction. It has also set aside regions, such as part of the Pantanal and large areas of Amazonia, as wildlife parks and reserves.

Many Brazilians are very aware of the dangers to the environment and one city in the south is trying hard to show us how to prepare for the future. Curitiba is Brazil's "green city". There children are taught to put some types of refuse in one sort of bin and the rest in another. Traffic flows smoothly along clear routes and special bus lanes are marked in central areas. Parks are plentiful and tended well, and flowers are everywhere.

It has been estimated that in less than 30 years São Paulo and Rio de Janeiro will be two of the most populated cities in the world. Yet overall Brazil's population growth is relatively low. But if there is to be a more equal distribution of the population, future governments will need to find ways to persuade people not to leave rural areas. This problem may be helped as the cities and towns furthest from Rio and São Paulo are developed, with their own airports and bus terminals, so that people see less reason to move to the coast in search of

◀ *Children in Brazil's "green city", Curitiba, are encouraged to take an interest in their environment. This is a drawing class in which the topic for the day is the rainforest.*

KEY FACTS

● Quinine, from the bark of the Cinchona tree, is used to treat malaria. To date only 1% of rainforest plants have been investigated, but scientists believe there are many other plants which could be used for medicines, perfumes, dyes, insecticides, foods, fuels, oils and other purposes.

● It is estimated that by the year 2025, Brazil's population will have increased from 153 million (1991) to almost 250 million.

better facilities.

Other problems that must be faced are the increasing gap between rich and poor, the huge international debt, and the need to redistribute land so that the majority of the population can benefit.

However, in many ways Brazil is a very fortunate country and compared with many others it can look forward to an exciting 21st century. Backed by its enormous natural resources, it is well placed to become a leading industrial and political force. It has also shown that it is well aware of its responsibility to look after the environment for future generations.

▶ *At the Earth Summit held in Rio de Janeiro in 1992, workmen put the finishing touches to a golden Tree of Life, shaped like a globe, and a symbol for the future.*

FURTHER INFORMATION

BRAZILIAN EMBASSY
32 Green Street, London W1Y 4AT
The Embassy has a good library and can provide pamphlets for schools, with statistics and illustrations in English.

CANNING HOUSE EDUCATION DEPARTMENT
2 Belgrave Square, London SW1X 8PJ
Canning House has an excellent library on Latin America, and the Education Department can advise on sources of audio visual material.

BOOKS ABOUT BRAZIL
Brazil (World in View series), Moyra Ashford, Heinemann 1990 (age 11–15)
Brazil (People & Places series), Marion Morrison, Macmillan/Templar 1988 (age 8–12)
Brazil (Countries of the World series), Julia Waterlow, Wayland 1992 (age 8–12)
What Do We Know About the Amazonian Indians? Anna Lewington, Simon & Schuster 1993 (age 9–12)
The Amazon Rainforest, Marion Morrison, Wayland 1993 (age 10–14)

GLOSSARY

BANDEIRANTES
Literally "flag-bearers". They were soldiers of fortune from São Paulo who explored and opened up the interior of Brazil in the late 17th century.

BIODIVERSITY
A new word describing the many different animals and plants living together in one habitat.

CAATINGA
A Brazilian name for a thorny sparse forest, particularly in the north-east of Brazil.

CERRADO
A Brazilian name for an area of grassland and low trees (it comes from "campos cerrados", meaning "closed fields").

COLONIST
A settler, or planter. The Portuguese word "colono" is widely used in Brazil.

ESCARPMENT
An inland cliff, or steep slope.

FAVELAS
Slums in Brazilian cities.

FEIJOADA
The national dish of Brazil, made from black beans and smoked meats.

GAUCHOS
The cowboys of the southern grasslands of Brazil.

JANGADAS
Traditional fishing boats used in the north-east of Brazil.

MESTIÇO
A Brazilian of Portuguese and Indian descent. Also known as "pardos", the mestiços now make up a large proportion of Brazil's working population.

MULATTO
A Brazilian of European and African descent.

MUNICIPIOS
A town or urban community.

SEDIMENT
Matter, such as rock or soil, which falls to the bottom of a river.

SERTÃO
Arid backlands in the north-east of Brazil.

TRIBUTARY
A river or stream which flows into a main river.

VAQUEIROS
The cowboys of the north-east region of Brazil.

INDEX

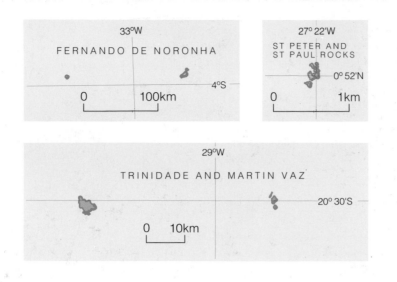

FERNANDO DE NORONHA
33°W
4°S
0 100km

ST PETER AND
ST PAUL ROCKS
27° 22'W
0° 52'N
0 1km

TRINIDADE AND MARTIN VAZ
29°W
20° 30'S
0 10km

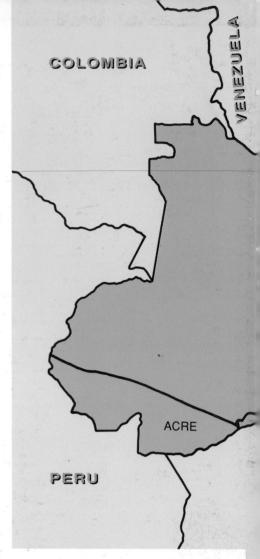

COLOMBIA
VENEZUELA
PERU
ACRE

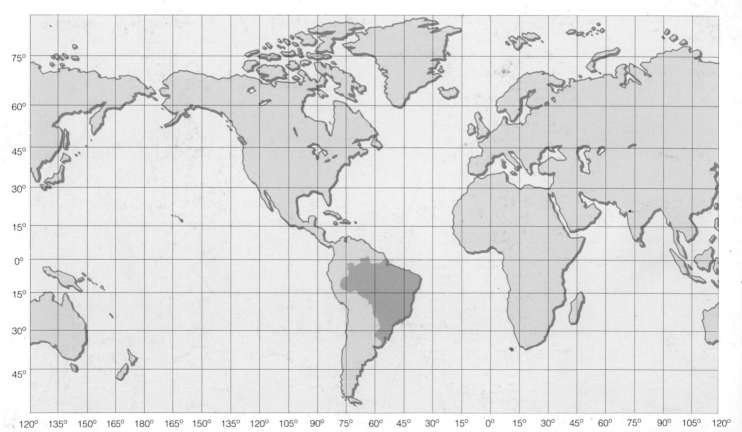

75°
60°
45°
30°
15°
0°
15°
30°
45°

120° 135° 150° 165° 180° 165° 150° 135° 120° 105° 90° 75° 60° 45° 30° 15° 0° 15° 30° 45° 60° 75° 90° 105° 120°

PACIFIC
OCEAN
CHILE